Sophie's Story

My Mum and Dad are getting ...

Lynley Barnett

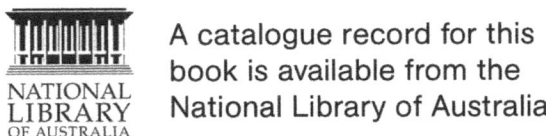

A catalogue record for this book is available from the National Library of Australia

Copyright Text: © 2023: Lynley Barnett
Copyright Illustrations: ©2023 Helen Iles
All rights reserved.
ISBN: 978-1-922727-80-0

Linellen Press
265 Boomerang Road
Oldbury, Western Australia
www.linellenpress.com.au

This is Sophie's Story.
Her parents are divorcing.
But that is not a word
that means very much to Sophie.
This is what she knows.

My name is Sophie.
I am three years old ... well
almost four really. I live in
two separate houses. Sometimes
I live with my Dad and
sometimes with my Mum.

Sophie knows that she stays with Mum while Dad works. Dad collects her on Saturday evening and she has a sleepover with Dad.

On Sunday, Mum collects her after tea.

Dad's house is new to her because he shifted, but he has made *a very special room* for her with a lot of her favourite toys and storybooks. She likes this because it means she has the same storybooks in each home, so the things she treasures have been put into both homes.

Her large Teddy Bear, her very special Bear called Beany (because of his hat), comes with her to each house. And just like Sophie, he is getting used to both homes.

She often "talks" through Beany because he can say all sorts of things that Sophie is a little frightened to say.

If you ask Sophie about going between two homes she will tell you this:

We miss Dad but we get to see him every weekend. Sometimes we see him during the week, if Mum has a Doctor's appointment or a hair appointment.

I have a big calendar on my wall so I know when we go to Dad's place. Every day I put a cross on it, and I know it is nearly a row until Dad collects us.

Dad has said that he will have us anytime Mum has to be somewhere. He sometimes comes over to Mum's house and he minds us there.

Sometimes he takes us out for tea and we get to choose exactly what we would like to eat.

Mum and Dad have promised us that they will try to be on time when they collect us.

Sometimes there might be a problem on the roads, but they will always ring and tell us if that has happened and Mum really does like that.

Next week Dad will have us on a Saturday and a Sunday. He is going to take us shopping for some clothes that will live at his place. We need gumboots for Dad's place because he has a park near us. But I don't think they make gumboots for Bears, do they?

I have two wardrobes with clothes, one at each home.
I need that because it gets cold sometimes and I have to have a coat to put on. Beany has all his own fur, so he never gets cold.

All my pyjamas at Dad's house are Peter Rabbit pyjamas. At Mum's house, they are the jamas with lots of flowers on. Dad's place has a pillow for Beany too.

Every Saturday I pick some flowers from Mum's garden and I put them in a vase for her. I put them on the kitchen table. I know Mum likes the flowers. She has to help me pick the roses though because they have prickles on them.

Sometimes I miss Dad. They have both promised me that if I need to speak to Dad they will let me ring Dad up on Mum's phone.

Dad and Mum have a picture on their phones which I can press if something goes wrong. They have shown me how to use it. Mum said, 'Well what if you accidentally left Beany behind … that would be a time you would need to ring.'

I will be going to Day Care Centre soon. Mum and Dad will take me there so they can meet the teachers. That way when I talk about them, they will both understand who I am talking about.

Can I take Beany to Day Care?

When summertime comes, I am going to learn to swim. One week Mum will take me to classes and the other week Dad will take me. They both have to help me to learn to swim.

Will I have two bathers, do you know?

I have two Grandpas and two Grandmas, but only one Grandpa and Grandma live here. The other ones live in England. I see them and talk to them on Dad's phone. I see my Grandpa and my Grandma, who live here, every time they come to visit. I love being with them. They take me out too.

Sometimes Dad and Mum get cross. I don't like that much but they always tell me that their crossness goes away the next day.

Mum said she is going to get a Cross Bucket. And we can all put our crossness in it. Grandpa said he is going to empty it into the garden when he comes over and Grandma laughed.

Sometimes I get cross but that is just because I can't do things like the big girls. Dad says I'll be the fastest runner, and the best netball player. He says that to make me laugh.

Dad has cooked me some funny dinners. One day, he set the fire alarms off because he burnt the pot. But nowadays he is much better and he makes a beautiful breakfast for me.

I have to learn to ride a bicycle soon. I wonder if I will have one at each house? They might be too big to carry in the car.

Mum is making me some crocheted blankets for my doll. And my Grandma is making some dresses for Bella (that's my Doll's name)

Dad has a project. He is making me a Doll's house. When it is finished he is going to make furniture to go in every room. I am going to be allowed to paint some of the furniture.

My Grandpa loves to work in the garden so he is teaching me all about flowers. And soon he will make a garden with vegetables in it for Mum. He says I can plant radishes because they grow quickly.

I do get sad without Mum and Dad being together but I like my two homes. I have two beds, two chairs, and I have lots of toys. I have a Mum who reads to me and a Dad who reads to me.

And best of all I have a bed in both homes that is big enough for Mum or Dad to get under the blankets with me.

About the Author

Lynley Barnett spent many years working in Perth WA as an A.D.R.P. (Alternate Dispute Resolution Practitioner) or Mediator to you. She worked thousands of hours in Mediation, with adults, couples, and businesses.

She wrote this book to help children whose parents are divorced or divorcing.

www.ingramcontent.com/pod-product-compliance
Lightning Source LLC
Chambersburg PA
CBHW051321110526
44590CB00031B/4424